soft magic

- Upile Chisala

ISBN-13: 978-1516967889

ISBN-10: 1516967887

<u>dedication</u>

for my loved ones, gone and living.

I am dripping melanin and honey.
I am black without apology.

Today and all days,
I am thankful for women of color
who love/write/create/emote
from the root
and never
apologize for their magic.

I want to think that God smiles
when a black woman
is brave enough to love herself.

now that I know
the soft magic of your laugh
and how your body moves like art,
why would I ever go back?
what was before you?

child of color on a journey to loving yourself,

if these poems find you on your saddest day
please feel free to eat them whole.

(they are yours, after all)

sadly,
when the ocean is your border
you must make do.
home is far
and your hunger for it
might make your bones ache.
so you study supermarkets
till you know where
to can find
goat meat
and
cassava
and
cornmeal
and
peanut flour
and
okra
and
dried fish
and
pumpkin leaves,
food that jogs your memory,
after all
you must make do.
I am sorry,
home is far and
you're hungry for it
and
the stubborn ocean won't disappear.

my father gave me math.
my mother gave me magic.
I have been using both to love you.

you are a woman after your own heart,
darling,
that is the bravest thing you could possibly be.

here you are,
black and woman and in love with yourself.
you are terrifying.
they are terrified
(as they should be).

my mother tells me she raised herself.
see……
she has always been both sunshine and rain for me,
I am in awe of how she survived and became a flower
with neither.

(for my mother, the strongest woman I know.)

I was intended for you,
lover,
what does the ocean matter?

all the lovely women living in your blood
are trying to teach you their soft magic,
please pay attention to them.

dark girl,
dream all those dreams.

I hope to do with words what dancers do with limbs.

remind your little girls with kinks in their hair
and skin as dazzling as the night sky
that they too are miracles,
that they too are warriors.
remind their little souls of the goddesses
they are always meant to be.

Fighting sadness is necessary war.

I write you poems because God spoke the universe
into existence,
so don't ever let me hear you say that words are just
words.
That
words don't leave a mark,
make a change,
create where once was nothing.

I must warn you,
there is soft juju at work in my thighs.

to the mothers
who fed us poems
till our bellies
had no room for
self-doubt,

thank you.

1. Do not accept the love of a man who makes you feel small, the universe is already so vast.

2. You are innately beautiful and completely irreplaceable.

3. You don't have to go far to find love and validation, start from within.

4. Boys are boys and men are men, tell them apart.

5. Be alone often, as you are, but don't let that turn into loneliness.

6. Remember to remain gentle.

7. Don't stay angry at the world too long. Seek out life in little things and move past sadness.

8. Touch somebody, with your hands or with your heart, with your words or with your silence.
Share yourself.

9. Celebrate your skin.

10. Be yourself and never apologize for being someone you love.

here, kiss me
let me give you the city I have been carrying
in my mouth.

it is when we don't believe we are enough for ourselves
that we start looking for people to drown in.

to the girl at battle with her body,

I pray you find a place to lay your weapons .

darling,
women like you are known to carry war between your
teeth
and still manage to slide soft words off your tongue.
you baffle them with how you fit both
battle and peace
in your body.

the trouble is,
some of us are terribly tender
and god-awful at picking lovers!
and it can feel like we want love
more than it wants us.

I am not sorry that we can't share a room anymore
without the walls tightening,
without the furniture sweating.
darling,
we created all this heat between us
we used to burn for each other,
remember?

please…
feed your sons the same softness you feed your daughters.

Little boys with sunshine in their giggles
are being mistaken for men
because their bodies were built like those of
warriors.

(for the moon-high baby boys of color who are still growing
into their warrior bones. You are little. You are loved)

'

you were born balancing languages on your tongue.
your family is several borders living under one roof,
bickering in the blood.
darling,
wherever you find yourself
you are foreign.

*rough translations

this whole ocean of a body misses you.
come swimming darling.
come swimming.

---

bwenzi,
ndine nyanja
dzandisambire.

sometimes I eat poems
late at night
when there's war in my belly
and
I've been tossing and turning
for hours,
trying to sleep you out of my skin.
darling,
I am snacking on soft words again,
you left me none,
you left me nothing
to fuel the honey in my bones
to wake the fire in my veins
you left me nothing
you left me none,
so I slip out from between the sheets
and feast on all the poems
you should've written for me.
all the poems
I should've written for myself.

dear lover,
I am sorry we can't pray away the ocean
that parts us.

When your grandmother dies,
she does not remain in the ground
or in the picture on your beside table,
you will find,
that when a man kisses new dreams into you
you remember to thank her for your face
and the lessons she whipped into your skin
you thank her for
making you worthy of good love
again and again.

girl, who taught you to be so silent?
to fold your opinion back into your mouth so neatly?

I remember the first time you fell in love,
you said even the water tasted funny,
and taking in air felt like sipping galaxies.
you looked at everything like you'd never seen it before.
this is the first time I realized that
love for a moment or a season,
can make an entire universe seem like it was just created.

you seldom know how to share yourself,
you are used to men
half-loving you
and not saying please,
so when he was all knees at your kiss
all plea in your arms
you didn't understand that a man
could coil so pretty,
carry such softness in his voice
and ask you so sweetly
for a portion,
for a place wedged beside you
and all your other thoughts,
you didn't understand
that your love was worth the beg
and how beautiful it was for a man
to become just bones and skin
until you kiss hope into him.

to the men who act like they were the first to ever love a dark girl,
I will say
'I have loved this skin since before you breathed on it'.

darling,
remember to run from men who promise you completion.
you are already whole.

fighting sadness with the bottle hasn't worked for anyone
in your bloodline yet.
so drop it,
make a warm meal instead.
wear something clean darling
and work on living.

before your hips came in
you were taught
how to be a woman
and
how much woman to be.

get in the habit of celebrating yourself
from skin to marrow,
you are magic.

your grandmother told you

"you become a woman the day you can take
heavy words
and
grind them till they are
honey"

heart,
tell me when you're ready.

too many earth-toned men and women
barred
and broken,
bodied
and bleeding
black and begging
black and barely breathing.

too many honey-skinned people
beaten
and burnt,
and bruised
and bibled.

too many melanin children being put to bed
early in tight boxes,
playgrounds and prayerhouses
becoming graveyards and tombs,

too many beautifully black babies
barely out of womb are being buried.

I am baffled at how blackness..
this holy blackness,
this sacred blackness
this blessed blackness!
has become a sentence
has become offense
felony
misdemeanor
misdeed
so when black blood bleeds it is minor
it is commonplace
it is expected.
so when black blood bleeds,
a system doesn't cry.

His kisses are love letters addressed to my soul.

beloved,
gather up all the hurt in your body
and tell it how you weren't meant for broken.

consider this:

your body is a blessing.
where it curves,
sags,
wrinkles.
where it was
scarred
burnt
touched,
all of this is a map of your life.
your body is memory,
some sweet
some sad
but memory nonetheless.
your soul is living
in a house of stories,
your body is memory.

you are the answer to a prayer I was too proud to pray.

you are beautiful,
and your wings are made of the things they threw in
your face,
the things that were meant t make you even smaller
in a universe so vast.
but you wove them together,
those treacherous old things,
and made wings.
What a beautiful creature you are!
What a beautiful creature you've always been!

I look like my father.
I emote like my mother.
    — how God dished out the meal.

sir,
for nine months you too swam in mother blood.
tell me, how do you manage
to hate a woman with every bone in your body?

darling,
there's no such thing
as a coin with one side.
I am honey
and lemon.

dear mother,
I hope to inherit all your tenderness
and the thorough way in which you love.

don't let the first time your daughter hears you're proud of her be at her wedding.

And today,
your bones
gathered your skin
and said

'Come on, let's do it again'.

Loving someone who doesn't love you back is thankless heart work.

the first time,
and all times after,
remember not to lose yourself
in the theory of a man.

If you are a miracle on thunder thighs
wrapped in sacred skin,
this is a poem
to remind you to stop and feel
the life traveling in your body,
you are many great things.
you are many great things.
you are many great things.

darling,
your strong bones were formed in a womb.
you started from softness.
you came from gentle,
please remember that when you love.

some days our prayers are twice as loud
and thrice as long,
some days they need to be.

fall for yourself,
shamelessly.

home is my mother's voice.

save some soft poems for yourself,
you need your love just as much as the next person.

try your best not to love empty men,
they are ugly in the mouth.

darling,
your body is not a burial ground for the insecurities of
others.

your mother asked you not to be soft,
she said your fragility
would have the men running towards
women who looked like they could unearth
mountains.
she said love was only for strong women,
women who prayed.
women who turned both cheeks.
women who understood
that men need and need and need
and want and want and want.
women who were ready to be less than enough.
she said there is nothing brave about a woman who
asks of a man what men haven't been made to give.
she told you that respect was in movies and kind love
was only in poems.

and you almost believed her.

Lover,
bring all your honey
and
all your hurt.

Tell her there are goddesses in her bones
and tales of triumph in her skin
and that blackness
is not a sin.

I am mine every time.

Trust me,
I know how to fix myself,
how to:
mend
and burn
and bend
and shape.
I know how to make myself something new,
so don't stay around out of pity,
leave me broken
and I will find my own way back to wholeness.

tell me
all the stories that start in your smile
and
end in your eyes.

choose happiness every morning like you would an outfit.

if someone hasn't called you brave lately, I will.
you are fighting sadness with everything you've got and for
that you are mighty.

To the men who loved me inconsistently,

I survived you.

feeling deeply does not make you weak.
showing that you feel deeply does not make you weak.
admitting there are parts of you that still smell like men who
walked into your life
and laid their sadness on your palms
and drove their empty fingers through your hair
and kissed you with their mistakes
and wrote you poems about nothing
and snuggled up to you with their insecurities,
does not make you weak.
they weren't the easiest to love, these men,
they tried to comb out their problems
over the sink of your happiness.

some folks are just cruel for nothing.

my darling,
you are the color of the earth
you inherited holy,
let no one silence the glory in
your bones
let no one make you doubt
that you
are
indeed
important.

how wild it would be if
we could actually make each other happy!

don't cheat yourself out of happiness,
you deserve all the damned chances
all the damned tries,
so darling please stop thinking of new ways to die.

darling
my blush alone
my blush!
my blush in itself is a hundred poems,
imagine
how much my body would write
if you loved me.

you will find that I have my grandmother's coloring
and my mother's heart.
honey,
I am inhabited by praying women.

you were the first thing outside of myself that I looked at and felt
connected to,
do you understand this?

He has found galaxies
in between the thighs of other girls
and suddenly the world
I was planning to offer him
just isn't enough.

she said :

"You deserve a full meal of love. Stop snacking."

you
and I
and all our vices.

What we give the gods in prayer
we get back in people.

your mother was a myth
your father was a story
but that never kept you from
loving mightily.

even absence is a teacher.

I now know that you're a wild thing,
I am sorry I tried to love the forests out of you.

Find a lovely thing and respect it.

poems ,
like bodies,
carry blood
and water
and bits of
everyone who's ever loved us.

love,
you wouldn't believe all the places
I thought I would find you.

he said :

are you sure you don't carry the ocean in your chest?
mountains in your eyes?
the sky in your hips?
because
you are starting to feel like the whole
world to me.

being this ebony.
having this name.
carrying this language in my mouth.
there are were times when I only wanted
to blend in
to sit unnoticed,
un-special,
but blending in is fading out.

sometimes I won't be honey-sweet
or love you with my softness
but please remember that
these bones have crossed oceans to find you
and they'd do it again.

Why are you so afraid of loving a strong woman?

maybe we carry our mothers' faults
in our bones too,
maybe our darling fathers' sins
are stifled in the blood.
I am sorry,
maybe we inherited some of their pain"

(what they carelessly gave us. what they've been
trying to take back)

kiss me all ways.
kiss me always.

when your quiet starts clashing with your lover's loud
and all their patient love is spent
and you're as much stay as you are go
hold your tongue
take a breath instead,
stop.
read your favorite book again
or
go for a walk or a run
or a smoke
or eat something sweet,
rest your heart a bit,
and for a moment
let love worry about love.

I don't want to be less me if that's the only way I'll get more of you.

darling,
I am a country you shouldn't go near.
I am at war with myself.

A thousand poems have been dancing in my chest
since the first time you
kissed me.

he says that

I add distance to distance
and am the reason why the ocean feels infinitely wide
time differences and seasons are all contraptions of
my hands,
because I am trying to prove
that I can break his heart
again and again
from thousands of miles away
and still be the girl of his dreams.

my mother's hands are tired,
you can almost tell when she hugs you,
she leans in and rests her fingers on your back
sharing a tiny weight in secret
unburdening, almost.

I am still learning to make language
out of pain,
to write out all the ache.
I am still teaching my fragile
and my strong
that they can co-exist.

when he offers you thin love,
don't take it just because you have thick skin.
Say no to loving a person more
than they love themselves.

don't ask him why he walked away.
he'll do the cowardly thing
and say
you were more war than woman
and that loving you was a fight.

I am still learning
the art of
give
&
take
&
rejoice.

Lover,
        we dug each other out of lonely places
        tell me that isn't magic!

sometimes it feels like I dreamt you up darling,
like I closed my eyes
and created you.

Denial, it walks in the family.

be careful with how you choose to love people,
don't destroy them,
don't destroy yourself.

current hobbies:
1. Loving the wrong men rightly
2. Loving the right men wrongly

bwenzi,
I know depression kicks you hard sometimes,
keep rising up from it,
you surviving thing you
you thriving thing you.

too many of us are oceans
with lovers that never learnt to swim.

the first time you saw him
you lost your language,
you swallowed your name,
and couldn't remember a damn thing about yourself,
this is when you shouldn't ran.
you should've made for home
before you spent
what felt like lifetimes
forgetting yourself in a man.

here we are,
black and in love with ourselves
and they spite us for it.

A final note:

dear sisters in melanin,
we need each other.

Upile is Malawian. She was born in 1994 and grew up in Zomba. She lives in Baltimore where she takes pretty pictures, listens to music and plans little adventures over tea.

CPSIA information can be obtained
at www.ICGtesting.com
Printed in the USA
LVOW04s0735230716

497482LV00028B/686/P